COLLEGE MONEY MAKEOVER

COLLEGE MONEY MAKEOVER

How "Abandoned Middle-Class" Families Can Cut College Costs, Avoid Unnecessary Debt, and Create a Clear Path to Funding College & Beyond

JOHN G. McCARTHY

perfectpositioncollegesolution.com

ISBN-13: 978-0-9978560-9-5

perfectpositioncollegesolution.com

Printed in the U.S.A.

Cover and interior design by Marisa Jackson.

DISCLAIMER

In completing this book, every effort has been made to provide you with knowledge on how to best address the multitude of challenges surrounding the late-stage college-planning process.

However, there is a chance that mistakes may have been made, such as typos, grammatical errors, or even miscommunications in the content, due to the complex nature of the subjects covered.

Please consider this book a general guide for you and your family in the college-planning process. Consulting a qualified late-stage college-planning specialist about your family's specific needs and questions is strongly recommended.

This book is not to be taken as legal, financial, or any other advice specific to your family. Any examples given in the book are exactly that, examples, and you should not rely solely on the successful situations of others.

Neither I, nor any advisor or organization who contributed to this book, are in any way liable to you or any person for damage or liability caused directly or indirectly by information in this book.

THIS BOOK IS DEDICATED TO
GEORGE AND ANN—TWO GREAT PARENTS
WHO BELIEVE DEEPLY IN EDUCATION, AND IN ME.

TABLE OF CONTENTS

INTRODUCTION

You love your children.

You want to give them every advantage in life.

You want to see them succeed.

For their entire lives, you have raised them with love and care. But you have also pushed them to study hard and get good grades. And perhaps they have done well in school.

Now the next phase of life for them is fast approaching—going off to college.

This excites you, while possibly making you anxious at the same time.

Anxious, because your first-born is leaving the nest for the first time. And, because you might not be totally prepared.

You have seen how high the costs have risen.

You have some money set aside, but not nearly enough. So what do you do?

Do you limit your kids' school choices to only lower-cost options?

Do you take on a bunch of debt to finance school?

Do you ask your kids to take on a bunch of debt?

Do you ask your kids to give up on their dream college because the price appears out of reach?

These are, obviously, some really tough questions.

And that is what this book is about . . . asking *and* receiving answers to what really works in the late-stage college-planning process.

In fact, I'll make a promise to you upon reading this book.

You are going to learn how to:

- Capture every last scholarship, grant, and financial aid for which your family is eligible
- Develop a solution that could not only pay for all your kids' college, but do so without having to sabotage or sacrifice your other financial goals in life

- Avoid making mistakes that could cause your family to overpay for college
- Pay for college despite not having enough currently set aside
- Pay for college without changing your lifestyle (don't cut up your credit cards, don't give up the family vacations, and don't resort to eating ramen noodles seven days a week)
- Send your child to their dream college for less than the sticker price, and
- Qualify for financial aid regardless of income.

That's just for starters.

WHY I WROTE THIS BOOK

During my time at College of the Holy Cross, in Worcester, MA, I had several good friends who were forced to drop out of college—not because they partied too much or were lazy, but because their families struggled to pay for the high cost of college.

I hated seeing that happen; when I graduated from Holy Cross I sought out the best late-stage college-planning specialists in the country and learned directly from them.

For more than 16 years, I have taken that knowledge and applied it to tackling the college problem for families.

This book is a collection of tips, tactics, and strategies that may ease the burden of college planning and funding for families just like you.

1.3 TRILLION IN STUDENT LOAN DEBT

That's the latest debt figure for college students in this country (as of the printing of this book).

And it's on the rise.

It pains me to think about all those graduates out there with a mortgage-sized debt strapped to them.

College loan debt is a financial epidemic in this country. A huge goal of this book, and of my company, perfectpositioncollegesolution, is to do everything possible to help tackle the debt issue by:

1. Authoring this book
2. Publishing the PERFECT POSITION COLLEGE SOLUTION™ Letter every week to give families just like you the tips, tactics, and strategies to beat the high cost of college
3. Conducting live college-planning workshops several times a month throughout western Pennsylvania
4. Offering free college-planning strategy sessions for families to help them learn where they are in the process, and to learn how to deal with and overcome challenges and concerns they are facing
5. Offering college-planning services for those who want some extra hand-holding

But there is also more that drives me.

My parents are like you in a lot of ways.

They wanted to give my four sisters and me every advantage in life, including the best college education money can buy.

But sending five kids to college, with three attending at the same time is a challenge—a big, *big* challenge.

And it was a struggle for them, at times, trying to figure it all out.

But they did. And if you were to ask them about it today, they would tell you that getting all five of their children through college is one of their biggest sources of pride in life.

Acquiring a top-notch college education, from a highly ranked institution with no college debt has tremendously benefited my sisters and me.

All five of us have done well in life.

And a great college education was a *big* part of that.

This is not just from a financial standpoint. College is a time when you grow into an adult. You are on your own for the first time. You are figuring things out, without your parents there to bail you out all of the time.

College can be a tremendous experience—socially, academically, and financially.

From a financial investment standpoint, studies show that those with a college degree have significantly higher lifetime earnings than those who do not. But like any investment, what it costs is a major factor. Any smart investor will tell you that. The money is made when you buy.

If you pay too much for the investment, your returns are limited. That's even more true with college.

In fact, what you pay for college can not only affect the overall long-term rate of return—your cost vs. your child's lifetime earnings—but it certainly affects your current life.

That's what these lifetime studies fail to quantify.

If you pay too much for college, and/or it affects your lifestyle because you or your kids are saddled with debt, then is it a still a good investment?

I was at the Apple store the other day and the young man helping me asked what I did for a living. After I shared about my work, he opened up about his college experience, saying, "I wish I didn't have as much in student loans as I do. My plan was to go to law school, but I don't want to add another $100,000 or more to what I already owe, which is $50,000. So I'm just working here until I figure out what I'm going to do next. It stinks, because I'd like to buy a house or do some other things financially, but my student-loan payments really hinder what I can do. I'm doing everything I can to pay them off as fast as possible. But it's hard."

My immediate thought was, *I wish I could help him.*

But at this point, it's too late.

His, and his family's, college-planning experience has long since passed.

But *your* family still has a choice. You don't have to put your kids in this situation and you certainly don't have to burden yourself with unnecessarily high debt.

Take the opportunity you have now and seize it with good, solid planning.

Whatever concerns you may have surrounding the late-stage college-planning process can be overcome quickly, if handled effectively, whether they are:

- Missing deadlines,
- Making mistakes,
- Not having the time to do everything involved,
- Developing a solid plan to pay for college,
- Doing something that will hurt your child's chances for college admission, or
- Doing something that will cause you not to get the most financial aid possible.

Use this book as a stepping-stone to help your children access the greatest higher education they can for the best price, and to develop a rock-solid college solution that will:

- Cut the cost of college,
- Maintain your current lifestyle,
- Avoid any unnecessary cash-flow crushing debt,
- Help you achieve more of your financial goals, and
- Give you a clear-path college solution.

The last thing I'll leave you with before we jump into the nitty-gritty is my mission, with not only this book but everything I do at **perfectpositioncollegesolution.com**. That is, to. . .

CONSTANTLY CHALLENGE
THE CONVENTIONAL WISDOM
ON PLANNING AND PAYING
FOR HIGHER EDUCATION AND
HELP 1,000 FAMILIES OR MORE
END THEIR COLLEGE
MONEY WORRIES FOREVER.

CHAPTER ONE

HELP! COLLEGE COSTS ARE OUT OF CONTROL!

It's no secret. . . .

College is expensive.

Very expensive.

And going up fast every single year.

According to its most recent survey, the College Board reports that a *moderate* college budget for the 2015–2016 academic year is:

> $24,061 for an in-state public college, and
> $47,831 for a private college.

Yikes!

But does anyone actually pay the sticker price?

Yes and no.

There is a difference between sticker price and net price for each family.

But, for starters, it's important to understand why the sticker price is so high to begin with.

First of all, what makes up the total sticker price?

Tuition
Room and Board
Books and Supplies
Transportation
Personal Items
\+ Miscellaneous fees

= Total COA (Cost of Attendance)

Sometimes the advertised cost of college doesn't include all of these elements. When you do your calculations, be sure to include every one of these costs.

Tuition: The dollar amount each college will charge to attend class full-time.

Room and Board: The cost of housing, which depends largely on whether your child lives at home, in a student dorm, or off-campus. Room and board also includes some type of meal plan, either through the school or through traditional grocery shopping.

According to the College Board, the average cost of room and board per year is:

$10,138 for a public school, and
$11,516 for a private school.

Books and Supplies: These vary wildly among classes, majors and schools. Some programs require as little as $300 per semester, while some colleges and majors are as much as $2,500 (with required lab equipment, books, and technology)

Average costs per year are:

$1,298 for a public school, and
$1,249 for a private college.

Transportation: This includes all travel expenses to and from campus (bus, personal car maintenance, gas) and round-trip travel costs, if living on campus (flights, turnpike tolls, gas)

Average costs per year are:

$3,215 for public universities, and
$2,661 for private colleges.

Personal Items: Most colleges include an expense line for clothing, insurance, medical care, recreation, disability, and computers.

Miscellaneous Fees: Any additional line items that may appear in sending the child to school, including social activities or spending money, fees for the library, campus transportation, student government, and athletic facilities.

So what do all these costs add up to at some schools?

Here are the ten most expensive schools in the United States right now:

1. $67,155—Harvey Mudd College (CA)
2. $65,860—Columbia University (NY)
3. $65,730—Sarah Lawrence College (NY)
4. $65,330—New York University (NY)
5. $65,965—University of Chicago (IL)
6. $64,519—Bard College at Simon's Rock (MA)
7. $64,325—Claremont McKenna College (CA)
8. $64,260—Scripps College (CA)
9. $64,224—Oberlin College (OH)
10. $64,132—University of Southern California (CA)

Just to name a few.

For ten of the biggest state universities, here is the total sticker price for in-state tuition:

1. $33,484—University of Pittsburgh (Pittsburgh)
2. $32,440—Penn State University (State College)
3. $27,812—University of Michigan (Ann Arbor)
4. $28,924—University of Virginia (Charlottesville)
5. $21,718—University of Indiana (Bloomington)
6. $25,631—Ohio State University (Columbus)
7. $24,278—University of Kentucky (Lexington)
8. $26,433—University of S. Carolina (Columbia)
9. $26,346—University of Texas (Austin)
10. $32,289—University of California (Los Angeles)

If you want to attend a public university in another state, you are likely going to see a *much* higher sticker price.*

1. $51,413—University of Colorado (Boulder)
2. $46,940—University of Arizona (Tucson)
3. $34,325—West Virginia University (Morgantown)
4. $33,916—University of N. Carolina (Chapel Hill)
5. $38,539—Virginia Tech (Blacksburg)

**Interesting Point: There are a few exceptions to the higher out-of-state public school cost issue. Some states have started partnering with neighboring states to offer reduced pricing for out-of-state students. For example, the Western College Exchange Program offers reduced rates among sixteen states near the West Coast.*

So, all told, you are looking at spending roughly between $100,000, for the average four-year public school, and $188,000, for the average four-year private college, which assumes your child graduates in four years.

Ouch. Unfortunately, it gets worse.

Now multiply these four-year figures times the number of kids you plan to send to college.

Below is an example of a family with three college-bound kids going to in-state public schools with the first child starting college in the fall of 2017:

	YEAR	# OF KIDS IN COLLEGE	COST*
	2017	1	$25,000
	2018	1	$25,000
	2019	2	$50,000
	2020	2	$50,000
	2021	1	$25,000
	2022	2	$50,000
	2023	1	$25,000
	2024	1	$25,000
+	2025	1	$25,000
			= $300,000

**No inflation added. Round numbers were used to keep it simple for example purposes.*

Below is the same family, but with private-college costs instead:

	YEAR	# OF KIDS IN COLLEGE	COST*
	2017	1	$47,000
	2018	1	$47,000
	2019	2	$94,000
	2020	2	$94,000
	2021	1	$47,000
	2022	2	$94,000
	2023	1	$47,000
	2024	1	$47,000
+	2025	1	$47,000
			= **$564,000**

You can see how these figures add up very quickly in a very short period of time for a family of three.

What makes matters even worse is that college costs are not steady like in these examples.

College inflation is real . . . and growing quickly. In fact, college inflation has increased a staggering 1,225% since the year 1978.

Percentage Increase in Consumer Prices Since the First Quarter of 1978

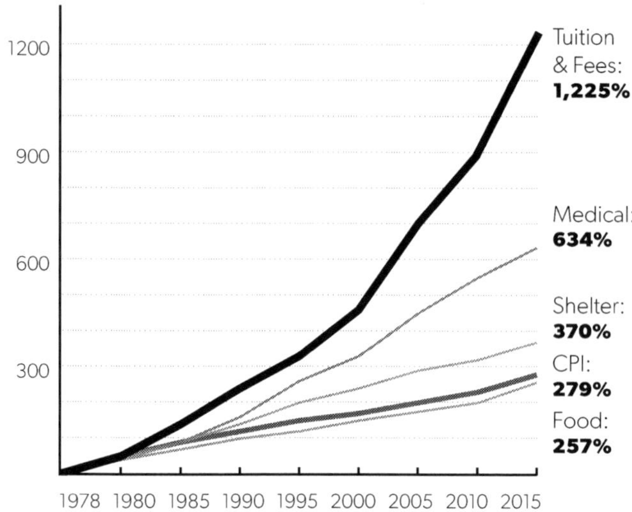

Source: Bureau of Labor Statistics

It should be pretty obvious by now that the sticker price for college is expensive and increasing by the year.

So, why are college costs so high and continuing to rise year after year?

There are several reasons—and one main one.

The biggest reasons are:

- Technology costs (colleges must keep up to date with the latest computers, lab equipment, software, systems to stay competitive with other schools)
- Real estate (new or upgraded facilities, dorms, etc.)

- Staffing (in order to keep or improve their rankings, colleges must attract and retain good professors)
- College presidents' and top staff salaries have increased dramatically
- Healthcare costs for college staff are up
- Pension costs for staff keep growing
- Marketing the college to increase enrollment carries big costs
- Net-pricing strategy (in other words, the *high price equals quality* marketing technique). Some colleges raise their prices to give the appearance that they are a better school. It's human nature to equate more expense with better quality. Colleges capitalize on this. George Washington University is a great example. The Washington, DC, school has dramatically raised prices over the years (without major changes in their product—education) yet applications at the school have skyrocketed at the same time.
- Guaranteed loans backed by the government. As long as you have not declared bankruptcy in the last several years, and at least one parent has a steady paying job, loan companies—backed by the government and the law—will loan you and your child every dollar you need to pay for school.

- College is a business. Whether it wants to admit this or not, a school's job is to persuade your child to attend for the biggest amount of money possible. You, of course, have the completely opposite goal—to spend as little as possible for the highest-quality education for your child. (This is why I chuckle when people tell me that colleges will help them with the college process. This is like going to the IRS to get your taxes done—it will certainly help you, but will it show you every tip, tactic, and strategy to get the best deal? No, of course not. Colleges are the same way.)
- But the number one reason college costs have gone up so dramatically is demand, especially at the top schools. There are *way* more applications than spots at the top schools.

Because of this demand, college and universities have no motivation to restrain price increases. In fact, a case can be made that the higher the sticker price, the more enrollment at the school will rise. More than a few colleges have made this part of their pricing strategy. People see a higher sticker price and believe it's a better school.

But in all this doom and gloom of price gouging, an opportunity exists for you. At the mid-tier colleges and universities there is less demand, which is a *huge* advantage for you and your family. It's also why school choice can play a massive factor in attaining a great deal on college. We will be covering this in more detail in later chapters.

CHAPTER TWO

THE COLLEGE LOAN TRAP

At this point we can agree that college is expensive.

So how is a family supposed to pay for it all?

Do you have a couple hundred thousand dollars set aside just for college?

Can you count on just financial aid?

Do you borrow money?

Do you pay as you go with current income?

Do you go to a lesser school—maybe community college?

Do you have your child join the military?

Do you skip college altogether?

Do you delay college until you figure it out?

My experience with this is that most middle to upper-middle-class families have some amount of money set aside specifically for college—maybe a semester or two for each child.

But after that it becomes tricky.

Even if you do have enough funds set aside, you would probably prefer not to use it all for undergraduate studies. That money could be better used for graduate studies, your retirement, or any other number of financial goals for your family.

If you have set aside enough to cover all college costs, congratulations! You're one of the few who have been able to achieve that goal. That puts you in the driver's seat. Use this book as a guide to pick up a few tips and strategies to help avoid overpaying for college.

But for the rest of us, who don't have enough saved for college . . .

this book could be a financial lifesaver.

College handled the wrong way can be a disaster.

Here's how.

Right now, unless you're one of the top 2% of college savers, you don't have enough saved to cover the cost of college.

We call this the *college gap*.

This gap is simply the difference between what college costs and what your family can afford to pay each year.

This is where the college problem rears its ugly head.

Good families, just like you, tend to make the easiest choice in order to fill this gap.

They take out college loans. These could be parent loans, or even student loans, or some of both.

College loans are so simple and easy to acquire. There are literally hundreds of different ones available, with the Parent PLUS Loan being the most popular.

And this is the problem. However, it might not become a problem in the first semester, or even in the first year of college.

You see, when you start taking PLUS loans the payments are small and manageable. *This is easy. I can handle this*, you say to yourself.

But eventually, year two of college arrives and you borrow even more money.

And that payment becomes a little less manageable.

Then year three hits and maybe you have a second child starting college.

Now those monthly PLUS payments grow even bigger . .

. . and bigger . . . and bigger . . . and bigger . . . with each passing year, until at some point you cry, *Uncle!*

Ahhh! you scream to yourself.

Our payments are now over $1,500 per month! How did we end up in this college loan mess? You think.

And that's how the college gap turns into the *college loan trap*—a trap that has ensnared so many American families.

This little paragraph from *U.S. News & World Report* nails the point:

> But parents need to think a borrowing decision like this through to graduation and beyond, before signing off on that first loan. A $20,000 loan for freshman year may sound manageable, but multiply that by the number of years you expect your student to be in school and the number of college bound children in the household and suddenly you owe $160,000 in Parent Direct PLUS loans, assuming you only have two children.
>
> That works out to about a $1,800 monthly payment under a standard 10-year plan. Parent PLUS loans aren't eligible for most income-based repayment options.

An extra $1,800 per month in payments would be really tough for most families to handle—not to mention it would seriously impede their ability to save for retirement.

So what's the alternative?

The best alternative is to develop and implement a rock-solid college solution early.

And not just any old solution.

The best solution pulls from a number of different sources, maintains your current lifestyle, avoids the college loan trap, and still allows you to sock money away for retirement and other financial goals.

That's what a good college solution can do for you. And what this book and **perfectpositioncollegesolution.com**, the accompanying website, provide—tips, tactics, and proven strategies to help you beat the college loan trap.

Don't be like so many families who take a Band-aid approach to this problem and do virtually no planning prior to college to help minimize the college gap.

This is the number one mistake I see parents make.

They assume they can't do anything about how expensive college is so they just wing it. And it's these exact kinds of families who fall right into the college loan trap. The problem is, once you're in the college loan trap, there isn't much you can do to get out of it. It's like quicksand. The more you try to get out, the more it sucks you in. It's a bad, downward financial cycle that needs to be avoided at all costs.

CHAPTER THREE

THREE CATEGORIES OF FAMILIES... THREE DIFFERENT TYPES OF COLLEGE PLANNING

So many parents just assume, *I make too much money, why bother even pursuing this process?*

That is a mistaken assumption nearly 100% of the time. Here's why: this thinking assumes your family makes too much money to qualify for need-based financial aid, and that there is no point in bothering with the process at all.

Well, as we'll learn in the next chapter, need-based aid is just one factor out of many in maximizing the late-state college-planning process. So by making one wrong assumption, you're basically throwing in the towel on the entire process. This will almost guarantee you overpay for college in some regard.

If you are like me, you hate overpaying for things, particularly when it comes to big-ticket items like college.

This could turn out to be one of the two or three most expensive things you'll ever purchase in your lifetime.

When you look at the biggest ticket items in your life, college is right up there among:

1. Retirement savings
2. Home
3. College education
4. Raising children
5. Wedding/engagement

So who can truly benefit from taking the time and effort to learn the late-stage college-planning game?

The short answer is that everyone can benefit from it. But how they benefit can be very, *very* different.

There are essentially three different types of families who are faced with late-stage college planning. Let's take a close look at each of these categories so you can see where your family fits in, what challenges you'll face, as well as some key things to focus on as you go through the *College Money Makeover* process.

Please keep in mind that these are general rules to follow. Every family's situation is unique. These categories are meant to give you a starting framework from which to build a solid college solution.

Category A Families: Income range of $0–$60,000 with limited to zero assets

What's important and unique to families in this category?

- Having opportunities to qualify for need-based aid at just about every four-year school (assuming the financial-aid process is handled correctly, which can be a big assumption)
- Filling out the FAFSA on time and correctly—a critical step in the process
- Filling out the Profile form, if required, on time and correctly—also critical
- Filling out any additional institutional, business, farm, supplemental forms on time and correctly
- Selecting colleges that historically meet a high percentage of need—very important (more on this in Chapter 9 and Chapter 15)
- Having a plan to manage any and all student and parent loans
- Having a plan to pay any out-of-pocket college costs
- Having an appeals process strategy
- Applying to at least six–eight schools

The obvious focus here is to take every step required to maximize the need-based financial-aid process.

Category B Families: These are what I call *Abandonded Middle-Class Families.* The income range for this group of families will fall roughly between $60,000–$250,000 with assets under a million.

This book is largely dedicated to and focused on helping families in this category. Families in this category are faced with the toughest task of all three types. That's because they get what I call the *middle-class squeeze*. They don't make quite enough to be able to pay cash for things, but they make too much to have need-based financial aid cover any substantial costs. In addition, if Category B families actually save money for college, they get penalized (depending on where those assets are saved).

To make matters tougher, the current system doesn't take into account any living expenses, which can vary widely depending on where you live in the country. If you live near a major city your cost of living could be two to three times that of someone who lives in a small town in rural America. Yet, the system doesn't take that into consideration.

That's the *middle-class squeeze*. As a family in this category, you have a choice. Either wing it and see how things play out—running the risk of overpaying or falling for the college loan trap—or be proactive with the process. Learn what your planning options are, minimize your family's college gap, and have a rock-solid plan in place well before your child starts applying to colleges.

Families who opt for the latter and plan ahead gain some tremendous benefits, including the ability to look your child in the eye and say, "Let's plan a trip to go see your dream school." These parents know with complete confidence that the family can comfortably afford that school choice—without taking on a mortgage-sized loan to finance it.

This can be an amazing feeling, and that is one of the many goals of the *College Money Makeover*.

With this goal in mind, what's important and unique to the college-planning process for Category B families?

- Having the opportunity to qualify for need-based aid at some colleges but not all schools (you will be less likely at in-state public colleges and more likely at private schools)
- Being in the trickiest planning category due to a combination of aid planning, out-of-pocket cost planning, school selection, and merit-aid searching

- Handling multiple children in college (this can be a huge bump in getting more need-based aid)
- Having a game-plan to pay for all college costs
- Avoiding high interest-rate and high origination-fee loans
- Having an appeals process strategy (Chapter 12)

Category C Families: These are high-income and high-asset type families, with an income range of $250,000–$1,000,000 (or more) and assets over a million

What's important and unique for Category C Families? Which steps should they focus on and which chapters in this book can help them specifically?

- Need-based aid will more than likely *not* be a factor—but not always—so it pays to go through the process anyway for a number of different reasons (Chapter 7)
- Still filling out financial aid forms, to prove they can't get need-based aid
- Maximizing merit-based aid—a *huge* key (discussed in Chapter 11)
- Taking advantage of every tax strategy available to increase cash-flow for college

- If you are a business owner, taking advantage of the busines-owner loopholes available to you
- Identifying colleges where your child is in the top 25% of the incoming class—critical to maximizing aid
- Having a game-plan to pay for college without taking on loans with high interest fees and high interest rates

CHAPTER FOUR

THE REAL TRUTH ABOUT SCHOLARSHIPS, GRANTS, AND MERIT MONEY

Quite possibly the number one question I get asked is, "How can my family more get free money for college?"

I mean, of course it is. We all want to have someone pick up at least some of the tab for college, right?

Right. That's why an important point to understand is that so many families immediately assume they can't get any type of aid because they make a certain amount of money or they have too much in assets.

And that is simply not the case.

Yes, some families won't qualify for *need-based aid* because of their income and assets.

But need-based aid is only one type of aid.

WHAT IS COLLEGE FINANCIAL AID?

An important point to understand is that financial aid is a system—just like the tax code is a system, and just like the legal code is a system. And like any system, it pays to understand how it works so you can take advantage of it.

With that in mind, there are essentially two types of financial aid:

1. Need-based aid
2. Merit-based aid

Need-Based Aid

Let's tackle need-based first.

Need-based financial aid is based on this formula:

  Cost of Attendance (COA)
– Expected Family Contribution

= Financial Need

Cost of Attendance (COA) is based on:

	Tuition
	Room and Board
	Books and Supplies
	Transportation
	Personal Items
+	Miscellaneous fees
=	Total Cost of Attendance (COA)

What is Expected Family Contribution (EFC)?

It is an income- and asset-based formula that determines how much your family can afford to pay for college each year.

There are actually two different EFC formulas that are computed based on information submitted through the FAFSA and Profile application forms.

The EFC number can change with how many kids you have in school at the same time.

With two kids in school, your EFC is split almost in half between the two kids, because this figure is the total for your family. With this in mind, one of the best financial aid strategies you can have is to produce triplets. (That was a bad joke.)

Financial need is the difference between the COA and a family's EFC. If their EFC is higher than the COA, financial need is not a factor that year. I say *year* because aid is given out on a yearly basis, and families' situations change. Maybe a second child enters college; maybe their income fluctuates—it all depends. So, it certainly pays to apply every single year—even if you don't think you'll qualify.

Merit-Based Aid

Merit aid is awarded for a number of different reasons—academics, athletics, and music, just to name a few. It is typically awarded from the school's own funds.

The upside to merit aid is that financial need is not factored in at all. So virtually any family, regardless of income or assets, can go after and potentially receive this type of financial aid. We will be exploring exactly how to do this in more detail in Chapter 11.

WHERE FINANCIAL AID COMES FROM

66%—Federal Funds

19%—College

6%—State Aid

6%—Employer

2%—VA Funds

1%—Private Scholarships

What jumps out from these stats are a few things:

- The majority of aid comes from the federal government (hence the importance of the FAFSA)
- The college's own funds are a substantial percentage and huge source of aid as well
- Private scholarships are a very small percentage of total aid, so do not spend much time or energy with them (Fastweb.com is a free resource that does a lot of the work in finding private scholarships for you.)

CHAPTER FIVE

FINANCIAL AID

Myths Versus Realities

Now that we have a pretty good understanding of how the financial aid system works, let's dispel some of those pesky urban myths about aid, once and for all.

MYTH #1: "WHY BOTHER APPLYING, I'LL NEVER QUALIFY FOR ANYTHING."

A lot of families think this.

It's the most commonly made aid mistake. Families assume they make too much and don't even bother applying for, or taking the steps necessary, to qualify for financial aid.

Bad idea.

Don't assume.

We see families with incomes in the $250,000 per year range, or less, get aid quite routinely. Incomes above $250,000 start to get phased out. But, even then, there are special circumstances that allow them to qualify.

It just depends on how the family is positioned.

It matters what schools they are looking at and where they fall in the system at a particular point in time.

An example: Let's say a family's income is $250,000. That alone is going to put their EFC in the $60,000 per year range—which will virtually eliminate them from aid even at the most elite schools.

But this family could have several overlap years with two kids in school, which now cuts their EFC almost in half for each child. This essentially brings the EFC per child to $30,000, instead of $60,000, increasing the potential of aid to $30,000 per year for the first child at an elite private school or some out-of-state public universities.

If both kids are at elite private schools, that's a potential $60,000 in aid per year for this family. That's a lot of money—and this opportunity will never arise if families assume they won't qualify and do not apply.

This is just one of many examples where assuming the wrong thing could cost your family tens of thousands of dollars.

MYTH #2: "I'VE GOT TIME, I'LL HANDLE THAT SIX MONTHS FROM NOW OR EVEN NEXT YEAR."

I don't know what it is with college planning (or maybe it's just human nature in general) but parents procrastinate fiercely on the college process.

I'll do that next year. I'll wait until next month. Let me think about it.

Bad idea.

If you have a child in high school right now, you're almost certainly behind.

Starting this year, the new FAFSA rules call for looking at income for the *prior-prior* year.

That means any income planning and possibly asset planning needs to be completed no later than midway through your child's sophomore year. If you miss the date, you'll have to start planning for the sophomore year of college.

The downside of this is that once your income and assets hit the FAFSA, or Profile, or Institutional Forms, it's not easy to get schools to forget they exist.

Freshman year of college-asset and income planning really sets the tone for all four years.

If parents really understood this, they wouldn't put off the planning process so much.

MYTH #3: "I HAVE EQUITY IN MY HOME AND A 401K THAT EXCLUDES ME FROM ANY AID."

The simple fact is, with the way the FAFSA is written currently, it does not ask for or assess your home equity in any way.

This means your home could be valued at $500,000, and the mortgage is paid off, but it will not figure into the formula whatsoever.

The Profile form—which elite private schools often require—will ask for this information.

Regardless, with good advance planning, you can position a large chunk of your home equity out of the formula. This could potentially qualify you for an extra tens of thousands in aid. So, once again, avoiding procrastination can pay off . . . big time.

MYTH #4: "THIS CAN'T BE THAT DIFFERENT FROM WHEN MY SPOUSE AND I WENT TO COLLEGE."

My spouse and I went to college a number of years back. I've got a handle on this.

I wish this were the case. Twenty-five to thirty-five years ago, the college-planning process was much simpler and college was much, much less expensive. *Ahh* . . . the good old days.

But that's long gone.

The price for college has exploded.

And the complexity it takes to avoid overpaying has gone up ten- to twenty-fold.

An unfortunate fact is, the college process has changed quite a bit. And it will take some effort, time, and help to get it handled properly.

MYTH #5: "THE COLLEGE PROCESS IS PRETTY SIMPLE AND EASY."

Once again—it used to be.

But with drastically higher sticker prices, billion dollar endowments, multiple lengthy financial aid forms, and a two-year look-back period, the complexity for college planning has sky-rocketed.

If you want to do everything in your power to avoid over-paying for college, you will take the steps necessary to maximize the process.

You could also ignore the issue, which will increase your chances of overpaying for school, possibly causing you to rack up tens of thousands, even hundreds of thousands, of unnecessary dollars in college debt.

MYTH #6: "IF I CAN'T FIGURE IT OUT, I'LL JUST GET HELP FROM THE COLLEGE AID OFFICERS OR HIGH SCHOOL GUIDANCE COUNSELOR."

"Isn't my high school guidance counselor going to take care of most of this?" That's what many parents say to me.

I wish it was true. Unfortunately, high-school guidance counselors are more than likely overworked and underappreciated. The average student-to-counselor ratio per public school in this country is estimated to be around 500 to 1.

It is not a guidance counselor's job to show your family how to avoid overpaying for college. They are not financial advisors or college-planning financial specialists.

Typically, guidance counselors focus on admissions, applications, and letters of recommendations.

And turning to a college financial aid officer for help is like going to the IRS for tax help.

They'll be helpful. But are they going to show you every tip, tactic, strategy, and legal loophole to qualify you for more money from their school?

Probably not.

In fact, their job is to do the opposite.

Remember, colleges are businesses. They have expenses, budgets, and projections, just like any other business.

Don't get me wrong, we still have to work with the aid office. But we need to see their role for what it is.

And their job is not to openly help you get more money.

CHAPTER SIX

HOW TO AVOID SCHOLARSHIP SCAMS

As a parent with a big expensive problem on your hand, you're a target.

Scammers and con-artists know that families in late-stage college planning are often urgently looking for ways to pay for college.

And because of this fact they will target you . . . if they haven't already.

You need to protect yourself and your family, and here's how to do it.

No matter how professional or legitimate the organization sounds, with names like:

> The American Association of . . .
> or The National Association of . . .

Be wary.

And if they ask you to pay money to get some type of scholarship or financial aid, it's a trick.

You should never have to pay money in order to get a scholarship or financial aid.

You could pay money for a college-planning service, or for advice, or for coaching on how to best position your family for financial aid. But to pay X number of dollars in return for X thousands in scholarships and grants is not ethical.

Be very wary and cautious of those who do.

With this in mind, let an article from Fastweb.com (a great, free scholarship-search website) be your guide to recognizing scholarship scams.

---

10 Scholarship Scam Warning Signs

These quick tips can help you spot a scam.

Knowing these warning signs can keep you from being a scholarship scam victim.

1. *Fees:* You shouldn't have to pay to search for or apply for scholarships. Check out the free scholarship search at Fastweb.com.

2. *Credit card or bank account information needed:* You should never have to give credit card or bank account information to award providers.

3. *Scholarship guarantee:* No one can guarantee that you'll win a scholarship because no one can control scholarship judges' decisions. Also, be wary of "high success rates"—they usually do not refer to actual award winners.

4. *No work involved:* You can't avoid putting in time to fill out a scholarship application.

5. *No contact information:* Legitimate sponsors should provide contact information upon request. If the sponsor does not supply a valid e-mail address, phone number and mailing address (not a PO box) after you've asked for one, that could the sign of a scam.

6. *Unsolicited scholarships:* If you are called to receive an award for which you never applied, be alert—it's most likely a scam.

7. *Pressure tactics:* Don't allow yourself to be pressured into applying for a scholarship, especially if the sponsor is asking for money up front.

8. *Claims of "exclusive" scholarships:* Sponsors don't make their scholarships available through only one service.

9. ***Sponsor goes out of their way to sound "official":*** Scammers sometimes use official-sounding words like "national," "education" or "federal" or they display an official-looking seal to fool you into thinking they are legit. Check with your school if you question a scholarship provider's legitimacy."

10. ***Your questions aren't answered directly:*** If you can't get a straight answer from a sponsor regarding their application, or what will be done with your information or other questions, proceed with caution.

CHAPTER SEVEN

THE FAFSA:

The Key to Unlocking $238 Billion in Aid

"You basically have to have a PhD to figure that thing out [referring to the FAFSA]."

—Arne Duncan, former Secretary of Education during his inauguration speech

$238 Billion is a lot of free money for college each year.*

Nearly all of it stems from one form—the FAFSA.

FAFSA stands for *Free Application for Federal Student Aid.*

It's issued and overseen by the Department of Education (www.FAFSA.ed.gov).

It's a web-based form that requires both the attending student's and their parents'—in a married situation—

(From the College Boards "Trends in Student Aid 2014")

income, assets, and various other pieces of information, with the income portion coming from the prior year's W2, 1099s, and tax returns.

There are just over 100 questions on the form, which might not seem like a lot, but here's what *USA Today* has said about it's complexity:

> The Department of Education acknowledges that the "volume and type of data required on the FAFSA can be intimidating and daunting for students and families." The 2009–2010 FAFSA lists 104 questions with another 29 sub-questions. "To answer just three of these questions, students must complete three additional worksheets with nearly 40 additional questions."

And the National Bureau of Economic Research's own study concluded that:

> ...the time required for tax compliance averages 27 hours per filing household, with time estimates higher for low- and high-income households. Ten hours per family is therefore a conservative estimate of the length of time required to complete a FAFSA: longer than the IRS's estimate of the time needed for a 1040EZ, but less than the 27 hours estimated by [others]. Note that our ten-hour estimate is for the "typical" family.

Key Point with the FAFSA: Everyone must fill out this form to get aid. There are no exceptions.

A mistake many parents make is to assume they won't qualify for aid, so they avoid filling out the form, and opt for more expensive and less flexible private college loans.

TIMELINES FOR THE FAFSA

Until 2015–2016, the earliest date on which you were allowed to submit the FAFSA was January 1, in the student's senior year.

But 2016 marks the first year families may fill out the FAFSA as early as October in the student's senior year.

Below is an excerpt from the Department of Education's FAFSA changes summary sheet.

Submit a FAFSA® Earlier:

- Students will be able to file a 2017–18 FAFSA as early as Oct. 1, 2016, rather than beginning on Jan. 1, 2017. The earlier submission date will be a permanent change, enabling students to complete and submit a FAFSA as early as October 1 every year.
- Use Earlier Income Information: Beginning with the 2017–18 FAFSA, students will report income

> information from an earlier tax year. For example, on the 2017–18 FAFSA, students (and parents, as appropriate) will report their 2015 income information, rather than their 2016 income information.

> ***Background***
>
> The FAFSA is the application that college or career school students must complete to apply for federal student aid, which includes Pell Grants, federal student loans, and work-study opportunities. In addition to determining eligibility for federal student aid, FAFSA information is used by many states, colleges, career schools, and private organizations to determine eligibility for nonfederal student aid. Completing the FAFSA is the gateway to accessing funds for college for approximately 20 million students each year.

In previous years, the FAFSA was available for applications to be completed starting January 1 for the upcoming application cycle, however:

> . . . many deadlines for state aid are as early as March. For some students, the current FAFSA application cycle is not aligned with college admissions application deadlines, which typically occur in the fall prior to the FAFSA launch.

As a result, time is a critical factor for applicants qualifying for aid. Finally, in addition to the timing of the launch of the FAFSA, the availability of an applicant's income and tax information may lead students—and, where applicable, their parents—to mistakenly think they are not able to file a FAFSA until they file their tax return. This may cause students to miss out on some federal, state and/or institutional financial aid.

In addition to changing the FAFSA launch date, the requirements for reporting income information has also been changed. Previous FAFSA applicants provided income information from the "prior tax year."

For example, 2016–17 applicants must report 2015 income information. Beginning with the 2017–18 FAFSA, applicants will provide income information from one tax year earlier—the "prior-prior" year.

This means that the 2017–18 FAFSA will collect 2015 income information. As a result of this change, more students and families will be able to complete their FAFSA using income information imported electronically from the IRS, using our IRS Data Retrieval Tool (DRT), rather than submitting applications with income estimates that may need correcting, or worse, waiting until the previous year's tax return has been filed.

WHY EVERY FAMILY SHOULD FILL OUT THE FAFSA (INCLUDING WEALTHIER FAMILIES)

For low-income and low-asset families, the FAFSA is an absolute no-brainer and is the whole key to maximizing the entire college-planning process.

For middle-class families who qualify for aid at some schools but not others, the FAFSA is still critical since it's the gateway to unlocking financial aid and the best college loans available, if your family plan requires some strategic college debt.

What is not so obvious is why wealthier families should be filling out the FAFSA every single year.

Here are the top five reasons why wealthy families should fill out the FAFSA each and every year:

1. *To demonstrate the family's ability to pay without any help.* It may sound odd, but this shows a school that the family does not qualify for need-based aid; therefore, their child might have a better shot at gaining admission. Most schools claim that they admit students on a need-blind basis, but that's simply not the case.

2. *To qualify for merit aid.* Many schools won't consider students for merit aid—which isn't based on the

family finances—unless an FAFSA is filed, proving they cannot qualify for need-based aid.

3. *To give kids "skin in the game" via federal loans.* Filing a FAFSA is necessary for students to obtain low-interest federal student loans.

4. *Because you just might qualify, particularly with multiple children.*

5. *Because your situation might change.* A job loss or other development could upend your family's financial situation.

TOP 10 BIGGEST FAFSA MISTAKES

The Department of Education is correct in stating the FAFSA can be tricky (they should know, they created it).

"A mistake on your FAFSA can delay the processing of your application by up to three weeks. One in seven FAFSA forms is returned due to errors."

—Fastweb.com

"The government rarely corrects FAFSA errors that reduce the amount of aid a family is eligible to receive. A few mistakes could cost you thousands of dollars."

—*USA Today*

With this in mind, I've laid out for you the eight costliest FAFSA mistakes to avoid:

1. *Including the value of a retirement account, such as a 401k, IRA, or 403b.* Directions state *not* to include these types of accounts, but a lot of families still include them. This is a mistake the Department of Education will not ask you to correct. Therefore your family could lose aid and never know it.

2. *Including the value of home equity when answering the question about investments.* Again, the directions state—not very clearly—to exclude the value of your primary residence. But you must include the value of any investment properties (with some exceptions).

3. *Waiting until your tax returns are completed.* This is the number one reason the Department of Education gave for moving up the FAFSA application date. Families were waiting until their taxes were done, which caused them to miss the priority filing date. Since aid is given on a first-come-first-served basis, a *ton* of lost aid occurred because parents waited to file until after their taxes were done.

4. *Missing priority filing deadlines.* The majority of schools award aid on a first-come-first-served basis,

so those that come in *after* get treated differently. And usually less favorably.

5. *Not filing.* I've seen countless families fill the entire form but then fail to complete the pin code signature at the end. Colleges will not get the information until this part is completed. Increases in security measures have made this step more complex.

6. *Over-valuing your business.* Business assets are excluded if you employ under 100 employees. A lot of families will mistakenly include business assets when they are not required.

7. *Lack of consistent information shared on the Profile form (which is required for most high-end private colleges).* Schools go through something called *verification* before they issue packages. Any inconsistencies between the two forms can cause a delay or explanation process. This delay, in some cases, can hurt the amount of aid families receive.

8. *Listing only one school—your top college—on the FAFSA.* Schools will see this and assume your child is attending that university (assuming they're accepted). But since you did not apply for aid anywhere else, they do not have to give you as strong a package. This also can significantly hurt your chances for appealing for a better package.

DIVORCED AND SEPARATED FAMILIES: WHAT DO YOU DIFFERENTLY ON THE FAFSA?

Which parent's information is needed on the FAFSA in a divorced or separated situation?

Moms?
Dads?
Both?
Whoever claims the child on the tax return?
Mom *and* step-dad?
Dad *and* step-mom?

Answer: whomever the student lives with more than six months and a day out of the year.

In a split-custody situation, where time is shared evenly between both parents, it can pay dividends to tilt the living arrangement situation to the lesser-income parent. (In the case of Profile schools, they will inquire about and count both parents' information, so this strategy will not work).

Also note: if mom or dad remarries, step-mom's or step-dad's information is required on the FAFSA. Fair or not, that's the way the system works. Plan accordingly.

Financial aid officers certainly have professional discretion to look at family dynamics differently on a case-by-case basis. And, occasionally, aid officers will adjust a family's Expected Family Contribution in these cases.

What happens if one of the custodial parents is not involved in the child's life or is uncooperative financially?

Once again, for FAFSA schools, it only matters who the child lives with.

But for Profile schools, that's a special circumstance and appeal letter situation. And each individual school may respond as they see fit.

CHAPTER EIGHT

BEYOND THE FAFSA:

Financial Aid Forms for Elite Private Schools, Business Owners, Institutional Forms, and More

Financial aid forms don't stop with the FAFSA.

The Profile is a separate form required by more than 300 schools. Mostly high-end academic and elite colleges require it, but a few elite state universities do as well, for instance University of Michigan–Ann Arbor and University of Virginia–Charlottesville.

A COUPLE KEY POINTS ABOUT THE PROFILE

- It contains over 180 questions
- It must be filled out online
- You must disclose info on your home, business, divorce, and custodial parent, among other things

- Filing dates depend on each school and scholarship
- Requires you to disclose much more detail about your financial life
- Will ask for retirement assets (but this does not mean they will be considered)
- Registration fee is required by each participating school—$25 for the first college, and $16 for each one, thereafter
- Administered by CollegeBoard.com

Aid available from Profile schools is *huge*. So it pays to get this form filled out correctly and on time.

Below is a list of the ten colleges with the highest endowment funds, according to *US News & World Report* for the fiscal year 2014. You'll notice that it is dominated by high-end private colleges that require the Profile form. So while their sticker prices and admission standards are very high, they can end up being some of the best bargains because the net price figure brings the actual price you pay way down.

1. $36,429,256,000—Harvard University (MA)
2. $23,858,561,000—Yale University (CT)
3. $21,466,006,000—Stanford University (CA)

4. $20,576,361,000—Princeton University (NJ)
5. $12,425,131,000—Massachusetts Institute of Technology (MA)
6. $10,521,034,492—Texas A&M University (TX)
7. $9,582,335,000—University of Michigan, Ann Arbor (MI)
8. $9,582,335,000—University of Pennsylvania (PA)
9. $9,223,047,000—Columbia University (NY)
10. $9,189,096,000—University of Notre Dame (IN)

These ten schools represent the largest endowments. But even smaller Tier-Two colleges have endowments in the hundreds of millions for the sole purpose of being awarded to students that they deem a good fit for their school, or simply to attract more enrollees at their college by tuition discounting.

ADDITIONAL FINANCIAL AID FORM INFORMATION

Institutional Forms: Colleges may require you to fill out their own forms with their own line of questioning, with questions that are largely duplications from the FAFSA and Profile. Colleges do this to look for discrepancies.

Colleges have a lot of money at stake with these packages.

Data across all forms—FAFSA, Profile, institutional forms—must be consistent. Numbers or information that do not match will be flagged, set aside, and delayed until they can be corrected or explained.

These delays can cause a family to overpay for college.

CHAPTER NINE

HOW TO ATTEND AN EXPENSIVE PRIVATE COLLEGE FOR LESS THAN AN IN-STATE PUBLIC UNIVERSITY

The Real Story Behind Net Pricing for College

What is the real cost of college?

Is it the sticker price? Or some other amount after you factor in aid, often referred to as *net pricing*?

If it's net pricing, are loans factored into that net price?

These are all good questions, questions we will be answering in this chapter.

As we saw in Chapter 1, sticker prices for college are very high and going up. This is bad. But what isn't bad is that discounts for college are increasing very quickly right alongside the rising costs. The only catch is that you must know how to play the college discounting game.

Here's what we mean.

If you can demonstrate a financial need, showcase some ability for merit aid, or get offered tuition discounting, the true cost, or net price, of college comes way down.

Let's look at an example of how this works for a family with a $20,000 EFC:

Lehigh University
Sticker Price: $62,498
EFC: $20,000
Need: $42,498

Lehigh Aid History
Estimated Need Meet: 93%
Gift Aid (Scholarships/Grants): 86%
Self Help (Loans/Work Study): 14%

The actual *net price* at Lehigh is:

	EFC:	20,000
	Self Help:	5,533
+	Unmet Need:	2,974
=	**Actual Net Price:**	**$28,507**

With $33,990 in free money covering the rest of the sticker price.

For this family, the actual out-of-pocket costs for college are *way* lower than the sticker price. This makes the affordability factor of a high-end private school better.

Now, let's look at the same family at an in-state public college.

University of Pittsburgh
Sticker Price: $33,484
EFC: $20,000
Need: $13,484

University of Pittsburgh Aid History
Estimated Need Meet: 58%
Gift Aid: 32%
Self Help: 68%

The actual *net price* at University of Pittsburgh is:

	EFC:	20,000
	Self Help:	5,318
+	Unmet Need:	5,563
=	**Actual Net Price:**	**$30,881**

In these examples, Lehigh, which is a high-end private college with a sticker price of $62,000, actually costs less than the public in-state university, Pittsburgh.

This same scenario plays out more than you would think, which is why it pays to know ahead of time where your family falls in this process.

CHAPTER TEN

FINANCIAL AID LOOPHOLES

How to Get a Fair Financial Aid Award

We learned earlier, in Chapter 4, that the simplified formula used by each school to determine how much in aid you get is:

COA (Cost of Attendance)
\+ EFC (Expected Family Contribution)

= Need

With this simplified formula in mind, how can your family take advantage of it and maximize the financial-aid process?

Just like a good tax accountant would help you find little-known tax deductions and credits that lower your tax liability, I'm going to show you similar tips and tricks for the financial-aid system.

In other words, what are some legal and ethical ways to increase the chances that your family will get more financial aid for college?

There are three strategies for putting your family in position for a fair financial-aid award package.

STRATEGY #1: ASSESSABLE ASSETS VS. NON-ASSESSABLE ASSETS

Both the Federal and Institutional EFC formulas take into account the assets that you have.

Some assets count in the formula, and some do not.

Here is a complete list:

Assessable Assets

- Bank Accounts
- Investments (non-qualified)
- Businesses (over 100 employees)
- Investment Property

Non-Assessable Assets

- Retirement Accounts (tax-qualified)
- Cash-value life insurance*
- Annuities

- Home **
- Farm **
- Household Items
- Personal Debt

This strategy calls for looking at opportunities to shift assessable assets to non-assessable assets.

For instance, both formulas will count 20% of every dollar your child has saved, in their name in an assessable asset, towards your EFC.

For example:

> $10,000 saved in your kids saving account
> at a 20% assessed rate
>
> = $2,000 added to your EFC

Multiply that $2,000 by four years of school and see $8,000 in potential lost aid.

That's no small figure.

Right or wrong, this is how the system works. You are penalized for doing the right thing—saving money.

Assessable parent assets work essentially the same way, just at a lower rate (5.6% is the current rate, as of the printing of this book).

For some families, it makes sense to look at shifting some of the assessed assets to non-assessed assets before filing financial aid forms. The FAFSA and Profile both ask for your assets as of the day you filed forms. This is opposed to income, where they now look back two years (starting with the 2017–2018 forms).

Should your family use this strategy? If so, which assets you should shift is beyond the scope of this book. It depends on your unique situation. A much more detailed examination of your family's specific situation would need to be made to determine if there is a good opportunity for you to use this strategy.

This is one of the big reasons I offer strategy sessions to families who read this book, attend one of my live workshops, read the **PERFECT POSITION COLLEGE SOLUTION™** Letter, or watch any of my videos.

During your family's strategy session, we look closely at how assessed assets could cause your family to overpay for college, how much they could cause you to overpay, and if there may be an opportunity to do something about it.

Visit **perfectpositioncollegesolution.com/strategy-session** to claim your strategy session today.

***Some colleges include home equity and farm values in the formula*

STRATEGY #2: INCOME SHIFTING

Beginning with the 2017–2018 FAFSA, families will now complete the form based on their prior-prior income instead of just a one-year look back, as they had previously.

This means that, for aid purposes, a two-year look back on your family's income will be taken into account.

The strategy here is that if you are contemplating any actions that might boost your taxable income, it may benefit you to accelerate those moves into a non-base year instead.

And vice-versa, it could pay to push any big expenses or deductions into a base income year versus a non-assessable income year.

Here are a few examples:

- If converting a traditional IRA to a Roth (which would boost your taxable income), avoid doing that in a base income year
- For business owners, delay equipment upgrades or purchases to a base income year
- Push to get any annual company bonuses before December 31, of a non-base income year

- Before the end of the year in a non-base income year, consider locking in any capital gains on investments that you had planned on selling anyway (especially if they'll be used for college)
- Work closely with a tax accountant to see how accelerating income or delaying deductions will affect taxable income from base year to non-base year.

Once again, which of these strategies will work for your specific family's situation depends on a lot of factors and is beyond the scope of this book.

We offer a complimentary strategy session for all readers. Go to **perfectpositioncollegesolution.com/strategy-session** to claim your spot today.

STRATEGY #3: STRATEGIC HOME EQUITY MANAGEMENT

A significant portion of Profile schools will treat home equity as if it is a resource to use for college. This means it can benefit you to be proactive about the assessment of this asset so that it does not count against you in the formula. Sometimes, a cash-out refinance can be a sound strategy.

However, using a cash-out refinance isn't without downsides. We'll use an example to look at both sides.

Family A owns a home worth $500,000 with a mortgage of $150,000. His two high-school-age kids are smart and perform well on tests, have a strong desire to attend high-end private schools, and have a good chance of admission—schools like Lehigh, Lafayette, and Bucknell (all higher-end private schools in Pennsylvania).

Family income is in the $130,000 range annually. Between home equity and other savings and brokerage accounts, their total includable assets are close to $600,000.

In the financial aid formulas, that $600,000 equates to a penalty of approximately $33,600 per year, or $134,400 for four years. But those assets could be moved to a non-assessable asset to improve the family's chances for more financial aid. At the schools for which they are applying, high-end private schools who meet a high percentage of need with free gift aid, this puts them in position to now pay $33,600 per-year less for college than before.

Now, the downside: cash-out refinances are not without costs. There could be an increase in payment, closing costs for the cash-out refinance, and additional interest charges on a bigger mortgage.

These factors have to be considered when looking at potentially using home equity management as a strategy.

CHAPTER ELEVEN

HOW TO GET MORE MERIT MONEY FOR COLLEGE

"John, what do you do if your income and assets exclude you from need-based financial aid?"

It's a great question. And one I get quite often.

The short answer—focus on going after every last merit dollar you can.

Here's how you do it:

MERIT MONEY STRATEGY #1: IDENTIFY SCHOOLS WHO USE "TUITION DISCOUNTING"

Numerous private and even some state schools now will regularly "bribe" students with high income and assets to attend their schools.

It's called *tuition discounting.*

And there are several good reasons for it.

Tuition discounting can increase the chances a top student will attend their school. Colleges get ranked and judged on how high the average incoming freshman grades and test scores are. The higher a school's ranking, the more applicants they get and the more alumni tend to donate. Schools will pay, for those students who help their rankings, to the tune of thousands of dollars . . . even tens of thousands.

Tier-Two private colleges are the biggest users of this approach. They do this because they do not get the same number of applicants as the Ivies or other big name private schools. But yet, they are competing to pull kids away from Ivy-League-type schools. They will not give merit money or scholarships, but they will tuition discount in order to bring the sticker price down considerably and to recruit top students to their school.

Tier-Two private schools and even some state schools have spots to fill at their universities. Families sometimes get caught up in chasing colleges, when the reality is—outside of a few top-end schools—colleges are the ones chasing high-caliber kids.

Even kids with less-than-great grades can participate in tuition discounting. In my fifteen years specializing in college planning, tuition discounting has never been bigger.

On the flip side, a few colleges took the opposite approach, getting rid of tuition discounting and lowering tuition across the board. Their applications and enrollments dropped dramatically. Because of that, the trend for higher sticker prices and more tuition discounting appears to be on an upswing with no end in sight.

MERIT MONEY STRATEGY #2: APPLY TO SCHOOLS WHERE YOUR CHILD IS IN THE TOP 25% OF THE INCOMING CLASS OR HAS A SPECIAL SKILL THAT THE SCHOOL VALUES

It can pay handsomely to apply to at least a few colleges where your child's grades or test scores are in the top 25% of the incoming class.

Many college admission and aid officers look closely at the strength of their overall applicant pool. If your child is in the top quartile there is a good chance that, outside of a select group of elite private and public schools, they will try and lure you in with merit aid.

Most colleges list their student profiles on their websites.

This strategy can also help with admissions.

I was able to use my football talents to get into an elite private college, College of the Holy Cross, where I would have otherwise been wait-listed or denied admission. But because I marketed myself as an asset to the school in a unique way (special thanks to my father for cold-calling coaches and sending out countless highlight tapes), I not only gained admission, but I also received a significant amount of financial aid to attend the school.

Another example: a good friend of mine used his football skills to gain entrance to Princeton University. Princeton is one of only a few schools to participate in light-weight football and he was an excellent player who happened to be under the maximum weight limit of 165 pounds. This friend also had elite grades and test scores, but so do the large majority of applicants at colleges like Princeton.

He marketed himself in a unique way and was rewarded admission at one of the toughest schools on the planet to get into.

What is unique about your child? And are there schools that will reward that uniqueness with money, admissions, or both?

CHAPTER TWELVE

THE ART OF APPEAL LETTERS

How to Negotiate Your Way to More Free Money for College

Senior year is here and financial aid award offers start arriving from schools. You open them and start asking yourself:

Did I get a fair award offer?
Was I under awarded?
Was I miss-awarded?
Should I accept the package?
Should I deny it?
Should I appeal it?
Or should I ask for an extension of time to review it?

All good questions.

And ones we'll attempt to answer in this chapter.

To start with, what makes up a financial aid award?

Award offers from colleges typically show up in the mail during the spring of the student's senior year. But in 2017, graduating seniors will be more likely to receive these packages sooner, because of the option to file the 2017–2018 FAFSA as early as October 1, instead of January 1, which was the date previously.

These letters will be comprised of several pieces of info, but mainly they will indicate:

- What the total cost of school will be for the upcoming year, by semester
- How much in grants/scholarships they are offering per semester
- How much in student loans they are offering
- How much in student work study they are offering, and
- How much in PLUS loans are part of the package*

**This is a sneaky school's plug-in that parents often mistake as a good thing, but let me assure you it is not.*

Once the award letter arrives, here is an excellent way to proceed.

STEP #1: PROPERLY ASSESS IF YOU RECEIVED A FAIR AWARD OFFER

We do this by looking at whether the award offer accurately reflects, percentage-wise, what the school historically gives.

Appeal Strategy #1: If the school historically meets 100% with 70% gift aid and 30% self help but they left your award offer short of those figures, that's an appeal point.

Appeal Strategy #2: We also look closely to see if the award offer properly takes into account any special circumstances with your family, which could be:

- Income fluctuations in base years. For example, asset sales to pay college costs may trigger capital gains that cause a higher income than normal.
- Higher-than-normal medical expenses
- Job loss
- Job change with lower income
- Disability

These are just a few special circumstances. Also, note that you'll typically need to provide adequate documentation of any special circumstance you're claiming.

Receipts, W2s, 1099s, tax returns, statements, etc., will usually suffice.

If the school did not take any type of special circumstance into account, we could appeal for them to do so. This has proven to be very effective in the past.

It's important to understand that each school has their own appeals procedures. And in my experience, you are better off sticking to their guidelines for filing.

Appeal Strategy #3: Are there any opportunities to pit one school against another? In other words, will School A meet the better package that School B offered your child?

A lot of colleges are competing for the same types of students to accept their offer and to enroll at their college. The key for this strategy to work is that these schools have to be comparable in stature. Meaning Harvard isn't going to compete with offers at Slippery Rock University in Pennsylvania.

But Harvard very well might match, or even beat, an award offer from Yale, if given the chance.

On the following pages are actual appeal letters used to secure thousands in additional free money for college.

Real Case Appeal Letter #1, on the facing page, resulted in an increase of $3,860:

Dear ████████,

Thank you for your time and effort in reviewing █████'s application. We are very grateful for your generous offer of $23,500.00 in financial aid and Stafford Loans. However, it is not enough for me to make up the difference between the offer and the amount needed of $17,412.00.

As a single mother, living and working in Los Angeles is expensive. More than half of my monthly paycheck ($4500.00 every 10 months) is used to pay the mortgage, utilities, insurance, car loan, gas, food, clothing and the general maintenance costs of running a home. Little is left over for any extras.

The cost of what I would be expected to pay for tuition, room and board, along with the cost of: transporting █████ back and forth between the west and east coast. books, and his other living expenses, would make it impossible for █████ to attend your school with the current offer.

It should be noted that the information from my 2010 tax return has recently been updated in the FASA. An amount of $20,000 is shown as part of my AGI. The withdrawal was made in that year from an inherited IRA to help pay living expenses. The money was mainly used to make our home livable.

No matter what, in order to manage any tuition expenses, I will need to apply for a Federal Parent Plus loan and Randolph College Plitt Loan. Any remaining balance would need to be paid through the TuitionPay monthly payment plan. My biggest concern is to avoid ending up in massive debt at the end of four years.

Randolph is █████'s number one college choice. He has been accepted at other schools (Hamlin and Knox), and we are in the process of considering their financial offers. But, █████ is most excited at the prospect of attending your school. He visited the school last summer and was received by Coach █████, who gave him a tour of the campus.

█████ was impressed with the campus and the personality of Coach █████, who could not have been more genuinely interested in █████'s academic and athletic plans. █████ would like to see himself at Randolph .

While I greatly appreciate your generous offer, I'm afraid █████ will be unable to attend unless his financial aid offer is substantially higher. If you would consider adding another $3,500.00 to $4,500.00 to his financial package, it could make the difference in my ability to make it possible for █████ to attend Randolph .

From everything I read about your school, I think it would be the perfect fit for █████. █████ is a hard- working goal-oriented individual with strong communication and leadership skills. He is extremely well liked where ever he goes. I am sure he would be an invaluable addition to the Randolph community.

Thank you for your time and attention to this matter.

Sincerely,

██████████████

Below, and on the following page, are the before-and-after results of a real case appeal letter that resulted in an increase of $23,568:

Carnegie Mellon

2014 - 2015 FINANCIAL AID AWARDS & ELIGIBILITY

Student: [redacted]
Date: April 03, 2014

COST & AWARD SUMMARY	
Cost of Attendance	$64,182
Total Gift Aid/Loan	$14,190
Remaining Cost	$49,992

AWARD ELIGIBILITY	
Institutional EFC	$53,910
Number in College	1

Cost of Attendance	Fall Semester	Spring Semester	Academic Year
Required Expenses			
Tuition	24,015	24,015	48,030
Activity Fee	123	123	246
Technology Fee	190	190	380
Media Fee	5	5	10
Port Authority	60	60	120
Room	3,640	3,640	7,280
Board	2,560	2,560	5,120
Orientation Fee	236	0	236
Subtotal Required Expenses	30,829	30,593	61,422
Discretionary Expenses (Estimated)			
Books & Supplies	500	500	1,000
Miscellaneous	700	700	1,400
Transportation	180	180	360
Subtotal Discretionary Expenses	1,380	1,380	2,760
TOTAL COST OF ATTENDANCE	$32,209	$31,973	$64,182

Gift Aid (Grants & Scholarships)	Source	Fall Semester	Spring Semester	Academic Year
Carnegie Mellon Undergraduate Grant	Institution	4,345	4,345	8,690
TOTAL GIFT AID		$4,345	$4,345	$8,690

Undergraduate gift aid does not automatically renew and must be applied for year to year. Graduate students should contact their department for information about financial assistance. (please see the information on page 1 of this letter)

Loans	Fall Semester	Spring Semester	Academic Year
Suggested Unsubsidized Federal Direct Ln	2,750	2,750	5,500
TOTAL LOANS	$2,750	$2,750	$5,500

Loan information can be found at www.cmu.edu/finaid/loans/index.html

REMAINING COST	$25,114	$24,878	$49,992

Student Employment	Fall Semester	Spring Semester	Academic Year

You may apply for student employment at TartanTrak after July 1st. Your employment earnings depend on your schedule and availability. These funds are not applied to your student account.

Additional Financing Options	Fall Semester	Spring Semester	Academic Year
TMS Payment Plan and/or Parent PLUS Loan and/or Private Loan	24,996	24,996	Up to 49,992

Carnegie Mellon

2014 - 2015 FINANCIAL AID AWARDS & ELIGIBILITY

Student: [redacted]
Date: April 21, 2014 (REVISED)

COST & AWARD SUMMARY	
Cost of Attendance	$64,182
Total Gift Aid/Loan	$37,758
Remaining Cost	$26,424

AWARD ELIGIBILITY	
Institutional EFC	$26,424
Number in College	1

Cost of Attendance	Fall Semester	Spring Semester	Academic Year
Required Expenses			
Tuition	24,015	24,015	48,030
Activity Fee	123	123	246
Technology Fee	190	190	380
Media Fee	5	5	10
Port Authority	60	60	120
Room	3,640	3,640	7,280
Board	2,560	2,560	5,120
Orientation Fee	236	0	236
Subtotal Required Expenses	30,829	30,593	61,422
Discretionary Expenses (Estimated)			
Books & Supplies	500	500	1,000
Miscellaneous	700	700	1,400
Transportation	180	180	360
Subtotal Discretionary Expenses	1,380	1,380	2,760
TOTAL COST OF ATTENDANCE	$32,209	$31,973	$64,182

Gift Aid (Grants & Scholarships)	Source	Fall Semester	Spring Semester	Academic Year
Carnegie Mellon Undergraduate Grant	Institution	13,965	13,965	27,930
Tartan Tradition Grant	Institution	2,164	2,164	4,328
TOTAL GIFT AID		$16,129	$16,129	$32,258

Undergraduate gift aid does not automatically renew and must be applied for year to year. Graduate students should contact their department for information about financial assistance. (please see the information on page 1 of this letter)

Loans	Fall Semester	Spring Semester	Academic Year
Suggested Unsubsidized Federal Direct Ln	2,750	2,750	5,500
TOTAL LOANS	$2,750	$2,750	$5,500

Loan information can be found at www.cmu.edu/finaid/loans/index.html

REMAINING COST	$13,330	$13,094	$26,424

Student Employment	Fall Semester	Spring Semester	Academic Year

You may apply for student employment at TartanTrak after July 1st. Your employment earnings depend on your schedule and availability. These funds are not applied to your student account.

Additional Financing Options	Fall Semester	Spring Semester	Academic Year
TMS Payment Plan and/or Parent PLUS Loan and/or Private Loan	13,212	13,212	Up to 26,424

Next is a second appeal letter before-and-after:

Duke University
Office of Undergraduate Financial Aid
2127 Campus Drive Annex, PO Box 90397
Durham, NC 27708-0397
Phone (919) 684-6225 Fax (919) 660-9811
Web Address: dukefinancialaid.duke.edu

2015-2016
Financial Aid Award Notice

INITIAL NOTIFICATION

NAME

Elk Grove, CA

Date: March 26, 2015

Email Address: finaid@duke.edu
Student

- Once you notify Duke University of your intent to matriculate, the Financial Aid Office will send information regarding accepting/declining/ or reducing the aid offered to you and reporting of outside scholarships.
- Please take note of the message codes (if any) for each award line. Each message code is explained on the back of this notice.

FINANCIAL AID OFFER

	2015 Fall Term	2016 Spring Term	TOTAL	
Federal Pell Grant	2,463.00	2,462.00	$4,925.00	PELL
Federal Work Study-FM	1,100.00	1,100.00	$2,200.00	WORK
Fed Subsidized Loan FM	1,750.00	1,750.00	$3,500.00	SSTF
Fed Unsubsidized Loan FM	1,000.00	1,000.00	$2,000.00	USTF

Before

TOTAL FINANCIAL AID $12,625.00

ELIGIBILITY

Estimate of Costs Billed By Duke:

Tuition & Fees	$49,498.00
Housing Allowance	$ 6,658.00
Board Allowance	$ 6,228.00

Estimate of Personal Costs Included in Budget but not Billed

Personal Costs	$4,360.00
TOTAL BUDGET:	$67,200.00

Duke University
Office of Undergraduate Financial Aid
2127 Campus Drive Annex, PO Box 90397
Durham, NC 27708-0397
Phone (919) 684-6225 Fax (919) 660-9811
Web Address: financialaid.duke.edu

2015-2016
Financial Aid Award Notice

REVISED

NAME

Elk Grove, CA

Date: 04/21/2015

Email Address: finaid@duke.edu
Student

> Once you notify, or if you have already notified, Duke University of your intent to matriculate, the Financial Aid Office will send information regarding accepting/declining/ or reducing the aid offered to you and reporting of outside scholarships.

> Please take note of the message codes (if any) for each award line. Each message code is explained on the back of this notice.

FINANCIAL AID OFFER

	2015 Fall Term	2016 Spring Term	TOTAL	
Duke Scholarship Trinity	23,180.50	23,180.50	$46,361.00	DUS
Federal Pell Grant	2,463.00	2,462.00	$4,925.00	PELL
NC Sales Tax Surcharge-Trin	228.00	228.00	$456.00	
Federal Work Study	1,100.00	1,100.00	$2,200.00	WORK
Federal Perkins Loan IM	2,000.00	2,000.00	$4,000.00	PERK
Duke University Schlp-Trin (H)	3,329.00	3,329.00	$6,658.00	

TOTAL FINANCIAL AID $64,600.00

After

ELIGIBILITY

Estimate of Costs Billed By Duke:

Tuition & Fees	$49,498.00
Housing Allowance	$ 6,658.00
Board Allowance	$ 6,228.00

Estimate of Personal Costs Included in Budget but not Billed (To be paid from family contribution, work-study earnings, and any other aid in excess of billed cost listed above)

Personal Costs	$4,360.00

Estimate of Resources:

Parental Contribution	
Student Contribution	$2,600.00
Total Family Contribution	$2,600.00

TOTAL BUDGET $67,200.00

DEMONSTRATED NEED $64,600.00

Appealing for a better award offer is not an exact science. There are no guarantees it will work. But it *absolutely* will not work if you do not ask. And while financial aid counselors might not admit it, they know that appealing for more aid at their school shows how serious you are about sending your child there.

QUICK SUMMARY OF WHAT WORKS WHEN APPEALING FOR MORE FINANCIAL AID

In the letter, be sure to answer these questions:

- Why does your family need help?
- What are the hardships you have been faced with and what are the problems these hardships have caused your family?
- What you would like the college to do for you?

Who are you appealing to?

- Financial aid appeals go to the financial aid office
- Merit awards and competing offers go to the admissions department

How to send the letter:

- Send via overnight or 2nd-day air FedEx (don't use any other mail service)
- Expect a reply back from the school within ten days
- If no reply, call the office to which you sent the letter
- Always be respectful

Key points:

- Be realistic about your student's qualities
- Make the facts about your situation clear and compelling
- Use the correct appeal channels (visit in person, letter, and phone)
- Be persistent (It could take up to five attempts to get results)

CHAPTER THIRTEEN

ZERO-DEBT COLLEGE SOLUTION

Year after year, college debt keeps hitting new highs, to near epidemic levels—$1.3 trillion as it stands now. Nearly seven out of ten college grads will emerge owing money, with a current average of $37,172.

That's bad. But there is a silver lining to these exploding debt levels.

Three out of ten kids are emerging with zero debt. Aside from having a trust fund or a surplus of wealth, what can a family do to avoid debt for college? This is a great question and one we'll tackle in this chapter.

But first, I am not of the opinion that all college debt is bad. Here's why:

College can be a tremendous investment. And it needs to be looked at as such. Like any investment, it should be well thought out, with questions being asked like:

- What are the real costs of this investment?
- What kind of returns can be expected over the short and long term?
- If taking on any debt, how will the cash flow on that debt be managed?
- How will the debt be paid off?
- When will the debt be paid off?

If the benefits *far* outweigh the costs and cash-flow needs associated with debt for college then it should be considered as an option. But not before exhausting all other avenues.

NINE WAYS TO PAY FOR COLLEGE

1. Savings
2. Cash-flow—parents
3. Cash-flow—student
4. Home equity
5. College loans—parents
6. College loans—students
7. Financial aid—need-based
8. Financial aid—merit-based
9. Grandparents

As you can see, six out of the nine options are not debt, while three of them are.

So which combination of these nine ways is the best for your family? That's a bigger question than this book can handle. And it is a *huge* reason I offer any reader of this book a complimentary strategy session to further explore which combination is best for their family.

To claim your family's complimentary strategy session go to **perfectpositioncollegesolution.com/strategy-session**.

TOP SIX TIPS FOR AVOIDING DEBT FOR COLLEGE

1. Take Advanced Placement courses in high school and use them to get college credit.

2. Take advantage of colleges that offer resident advisor programs. Many of these programs cover the cost of room and board. This is essentially tax-free income for the student, which typically will not affect any additional financial aid award money.

3. Maximize any need-based and merit-based financial aid opportunities.

4. Have a plan to graduate in four years or less.

5. Save money before college. There is nothing fancy about this one. Just be diligent about structuring

your budget and being efficient with managing your cash flow. Setting up an automatic savings program can be extremely beneficial, no matter how small.

6. Have a set cash-flow amount that both parents and students can realistically contribute towards college, without sacrificing lifestyle.

SHOULD YOU HAVE YOUR KIDS PARTICIPATE IN PAYING FOR COLLEGE?

Yes. Studies show students actually perform better at college if they have some "skin in the game."

A study done by University of California Professor Laura Hamilton shows a larger contribution from parents are linked to lower grades among students at four-year colleges. These results are surprising, in that you would assume kids would achieve better grades without having to work. You would think more study time equals better grades, wouldn't it?

On the contrary, kids who receive more money from parents and do not have to budget their time between study and work have more free time. And they use this free time to engage in leisure activities—partying, in all likelihood. When you think about this, it makes sense. College is the first time kids are on their own without a lot of structure to their day, outside of classroom work. This is way different than high school, which has a very regimented daily structure to it. When kids are now suddenly given this dramatic increase in free time, combined with basically zero parental oversight, it's easy to see how they end up losing focus on their studies.

CHAPTER FOURTEEN

COLLEGE SELECTION MASTERY

What is the best school for my child?

How do I pick the best school from among 4,000-plus accredited colleges?

The short answer is that there is no 100% exact science on picking the right school for your child.

However, there are three factors that are present for all kids—and their parents—who have a great experience at college.

These three factors are that the school they attend is:

1. A good fit academically
2. A good fit financially
3. A good fit socially

Connect on all three of these factors and it's almost a guarantee that you and your child—as long as they do their part in school—will have a great college experience.

But miss any one of these three factors and bad things can happen:

- If your child has to change majors or schools because the program they started in wasn't the right fit and the second and third choice are not offered at that school—that's a problem. Now instead of four years of undergrad, it's five or six years your family is paying for.
- If your family quickly becomes saddled with high-interest and high-origination-fee loans—that's a problem. Payments on college loans can escalate quickly and spiral out of control with little to no chance of recovery.
- If your child is miserable socially, not having fun or connecting with other students—that's a problem. This can lead to kids dropping out, or worse, resorting to destructive behaviors such as excessive drinking, hanging with the wrong crowd, or drugs.

So how do you and your child find the school with the right academic, social, and financial fit?

STEP #1: EXPLORE THE RIGHT-FIT CAREER PATH(S) FOR YOUR CHILD WELL BEFORE SELECTING A COLLEGE

This is easier said than done.

What do you want to do with the rest of your life?

Answering this tough question can be a daunting task for people of all ages, especially for a 15- to 17-year-old.

The human brain—frontal cortex, specifically—does not fully develop until age 25.

This explains why teenagers are prone to such erratic behavior at times; they are, literally, working with roughly half of a brain at this point in their lives.

With these biological facts in mind, it makes little sense that we're asking our kids to make, without good tools and guidance, very tough decisions about what they want to do for the rest of their life.

Kids are faced with making career decisions with little or no help.

No wonder so many kids struggle unnecessarily in college.

It can be difficult at college to adapt to new surroundings without day-to-day help from parents, and then on top of that, to realize that maybe the major and career path they chose was the wrong one.

Fortunately, today there are some great tools and resources available to help kids in the process of making major decisions, such as choosing a career. But this a *much* bigger topic that cannot be adequately covered in this book.

Here is another large benefit of the complimentary strategy session you receive with this book. We look for potential deficiencies in your child's college major, school choices, and chosen career path, and explore some tremendously helpful tools and resources that are available to help you and your child with this part of the college process.

Visit **perfectpositioncollegesolution.com/strategy-session** now to secure your college funding strategy session.

STEP #2: IDENTIFYING AND PICKING THE RIGHT-FIT/RIGHT-PRICE COLLEGE

We've discussed in-depth in previous chapters why having an estimate of the net price for each school ahead of time is so important (Chapter 9). But that's not all you need to know.

Some other things to ask when searching for the right-fit/right-price college:

- What are the school's overall graduation rates?

- What are the school's four-year graduation rates?
- What is the average number of years it takes kids to graduate at that college?

Here are four-year graduation rates at a random selection of private colleges (data from the College Board):

88%—University of Pennsylvania
87%—Bucknell (PA)
86%—Lafayette (PA)
78%—Franklin and Marshal (PA)
71%—Allegheny College (PA)
68%—Mount St. Mary's University (MD)
65%—John Carroll University (OH)

And here is a sampling of four-year graduation rates at several public universities (data from the College Board):

72%—University of Michigan (Main Campus)
63%—University of Delaware (Main Campus)
62%—University of Penn State (Main Campus)
59%—University of Pittsburgh (Main Campus)
47%—Ohio University (Main Campus)
34%—University of Arizona (Main Campus)
32%—West Virginia University (Main Campus)

When picking schools, these statistics matter. Applying to schools with high four-year graduation rates stack the deck in your child's favor to do the same. But if your child has to take just one extra semester to graduate college, that can potentially cost your family tens of thousands of dollars.

CHAPTER FIFTEEN

THE UGLY TRUTH ABOUT GRADUATION RATES...

And What to Do About It

"The vast majority of kids who enter public universities do not graduate on time. Only 19% of full-time students earn a bachelor's degree in four years."

—*New York Times*, reporting on an independent study called The Four-Year Myth

The report cited several main reasons for lag times on graduation:

- Inability to register for required courses
- Credits lost in transfer
- Remediation sequences that do not work
- Students taking too few credits per semester to finish on time

> …it is costing students and their parents billions of extra dollars.
>
> Tuition borrowers who do not graduate on time take on far more debt in their extra years. According to data from Temple University in Philadelphia and from the University of Texas, Austin, two extra years on campus increases debt by nearly 70 percent.

So what's a family to do? And does this affect private colleges the same way?

One of the best strategies for making college affordable and for boosting graduation rates overall is to ensure that many more students graduate on time.

Look at historical graduation rates before attending schools, which we saw in both public and private schools in Chapter 14. These will be a tremendous indicator of whether your child will get in and out promptly.

With a few exceptions, your child has a much better shot at completing their degree in four years at a private college. The main reason being that private institutions typically have smaller class sizes and fewer over-enrollment issues, which continue to plague public schools.

But simply choosing a school with higher-than-average four-year graduate rates is not the only thing you can do to get your child in and out in four years or less.

SEVEN WAYS TO HELP YOUR CHILD GRADUATE IN FOUR YEARS OR LESS AT PUBLIC OR PRIVATE COLLEGES

1. *Choose a major early on.* This is where prep work prior to college can pay huge dividends. By going into college with a definite major, your child will stack the deck towards graduating on time. This assumes they stick with that major and do not switch multiple times.

2. *Take classes over the summer.* This can be the perfect time to catch up or get ahead on those general requirements that my have slipped by the wayside during the year. Bonus points if these classes can be taken at a less expensive community college, or other four-year school, and are allowed to transfer in.

3. *Manage class schedule wisely.* Avoid under-water-basket-weaving-type courses, or fluff courses, as I call them, and stick to the core curriculum needed for prerequisites and your major.

4. *Stay on pace, or ahead, with credits each semester.* The temptation can arise to take it easy on credits or course-load for a semester or two. Avoid this at all costs. This will almost surely push your child off-track from the four-year graduation pace.

5. *Use high school AP credits to count for college credit.* A high percentage of colleges allow Advanced Placement taken in high school to count toward college credit, but usually with some process each school wants you to go through in order to get them counted. For time and money's sake, it is well worth the trouble to shave off a few classes of college.

6. *Be proactive about registration.* "The early bird gets the worm" applies here. Procrastination and hesitation may cause you to miss out on getting into the classes they need to fill their requirements. On the first day classes open—better yet the hour they open—be ready to pounce on the classes you need.

7. *Look for "four-year graduation guarantees."* An increasing number of colleges are offering these types of agreements. The terms and conditions vary, but the general idea is that you have to declare a major in your first semester or first year and then stick with it. And if, for some reason, you cannot get a class because of over-scheduling at the school, a substitute course will be approved, or the school will waive the class requirement, or pay the tuition.

CHAPTER SIXTEEN

PERFECT POSITION COLLEGE SOLUTION™

A Proven Five-Step System for College-Funding Success

At this point, you now possess in your hands tools, tactics, and strategies on how to win the college money game. You also have a play-book on how to avoid the biggest money and time sucking mistakes that plague so many parents with college-bound kids. But it's not enough just to possess this information. You must put it to use.

While this book is more general in nature and not specific to any particular family, it is a great starting point for you and your family.

My hope is that this starting point is the beginning of a very successful journey on your family's path to college.

And like any journey it helps to have a guide. Let the PERFECT POSITION COLLEGE SOLUTION™ and it's five pillars of college-funding success be your guide:

PILLAR #1: AVOID THE COLLEGE LOAN TRAP

One of the great financial epidemics of modern times is the college loan bubble. And yet so many families (both parents and kids) resort to college loans to fund college.

Of all the college loans available PLUS loans are the most popular among parents. Despite being expensive (typically 2–3% higher than mortgage rates), and a 4.2% origination fee is tacked on for every dollar you borrow.

Ouch!

So, if it's such a bad deal, why do so families fall for PLUS loans and the college debt trap?

Two main reasons:

1. Most colleges include PLUS loans in their financial aid packages, which gives the subtle appearance that the school is suggesting you take them.
2. PLUS loans are easy to get and qualify for. Simply fill out an application of a few pages online and wait for approval. As long as you haven't filed for bankruptcy in the past year, you can pretty much borrow every dollar you'll ever need for college with them.

Obviously, going down the PLUS loan path is a bad deal. And should be avoided at nearly all costs.

How your family handles this potential college-loan trap situation is the number-one key to getting your child in and out of college without resorting to any potential cash-flow crushing college loans. When you add the origination fees and interest costs together, they can add 50% or more to the already insanely high sticker price of college.

PILLAR #2: POSITION FOR MAXIMUM FINANCIAL AID

Even if you bring in a healthy six-figure income, there could still be significant money available for your family if you play the financial-aid game right. Identify, apply for, and focus on schools that historically meet a high percentage of need with gift aid. Avoid schools that meet a low percentage of need or who meet need with a high percentage of self-help.

PILLAR #3: MAINTAIN MONTHLY LIFESTYLE

There is a popular belief that in order to fund college, you should cut spending to the bone, eat ramen noodles regularly, eliminate family vacations, and cut up your credit cards. While this type of scarcity mentality approach to paying for college might work in the short term, eventually families crack because it's just not realistic. Nor is it necessary (for the large majority of families). Although on some occasions, families are in need of reigning in their spending and need help with a budget.

It's also unnecessary and ill advised to go the PLUS loan route. We've stated our reasons why in Pillar #1. But there is another major reason PLUS loans don't work—the monthly payments. At first they appear manageable —$150/mo or so in year one. But then year two and three hit and more loans pile on. Then the second child enters college. And before you know it, you've taken out $150,000 for college and the monthly payments are more than your mortgage. Yikes!

This is *never* a good option.

There is always a better way. Typically that way involves looking at your current finances and positioning your assets and cash-flow in a way that frees up money to fund college without changing your lifestyle at all.

PILLAR #4: PREDICTABLE AND SAFE WAY TO PAY FOR COLLEGE

This pillar involves developing a customized solution that could help your family:

- Pay for college without changing your lifestyle.

- Avoid unnecessary and high interest college debt.
- Increase your eligibility for financial aid (both need-based and merit-based).
- Keep your retirement and other long term financial goals in line and on track.

How to achieve Pillar #4 is often as simple as taking your current situation and making it more efficient. However, this process isn't always so obvious. Sometimes it takes a specialist with a fresh set of eyes to look beyond the way you've always done things.

As part of this step, we also recommend using a tool we call The Original College Savings Stress Test. This tool gives you a side-by-side comparison of how each financial vehicle stacks up to one another. Making it much easier to select the best one.

During the financial crisis of 2008, where numerous college savings accounts took *huge* losses, this tool proved invaluable.

Instead of having large portions of college savings in risk assets, The Original College Savings Stress Test showed families other options that guaranteed the principle of their accounts.

But having strong guarantees is just one of the characteristics that work best in this situation. A full list includes:

- Guarantees
- Liquidity
- Tax-advantages
- Competitive interest rate
- Exempt from the financial aid formula

PILLAR #5: POSITION FOR LONG-TERM FINANCIAL SUCCESS

For alot of families, the college problem is actually not just about college. It can also be just as much about retirement.

College is the last major expense most parents face just before retirement and despite parent's best efforts they could be off course to hit either their college and/or retirement goals.

With this in mind, ask yourself these questions:

- Are you on track to retire at the age you want?
- Can you retire *and* fund college without sticking your child with a mortgage-sized college loan?

- What kind of income will your assets be able to generate at retirement time?
- Is there a way to have more certainty and less risk with your financial future?
- Is it possible to position your assets for upside gains of the market, with no downside risk?

If you answer "no" to anyone of these questions, consider making Pillar #5 a priority in your family's PERFECT POSITION COLLEGE SOLUTION.™

APPENDIX

Resources for Your Family's College-Planning Journey

THE PERFECT POSITION COLLEGE SOLUTION™ LETTER:

Subscribe for free at **perfectpositioncollegesolution.com**

COLLEGE FUNDING STRATEGY SESSION:

Take advantage of one of these, when available, by going to **perfectpositioncollegesolution.com/strategy-session**

SERVICES FOR FAMILIES WHO ARE A GREAT FIT:

Education Services:

- Personalized private student interview
- Student assessment
    1. Personality profile evaluation
    2. Advanced search of careers, majors & studies based on specific student interests

3. Innovative college search based on demographics and personalized areas of importance

4. SAT + ACT test prep personalized online test prep solutions to help students score at their highest potential

College Funding Strategies:

- Calculate your expected family contribution (EFC)
- Planning recommendations on how to reduce the EFC
- Financial aid award estimates for the schools of your choice and recommendations for additional schools to be considered
- Recommendations to pay your EFC on a tax-favored basis
- A customized PERFECT POSITION COLLEGE SOLUTION™ for your family: A complete overview on college funding, cash-flow, and long-term financial goals—with guidance on how to improve each area
- Merit-based financial aid search: Identifying which schools will award the most merit money with your student's GPA, test scores, and majors of interest

Financial Aid Data Gathering & Processing:

- Complete the Free Application for Federal Student Aid Application (FAFSA)
- Confirm the accuracy of the Student Aid Report (SAR)
- Register and complete the CSS Profile, if necessary
- Complete any additional forms required by schools, when applicable
- Spreadsheet evaluation of all award letters to ensure a fair award offer
- Oversee the award letter appeal process with tested and proven negotiation strategies

Value-Added Services:

- College funding tips of the week
- Phone and email support for both parents and students
- Personalized one-on-one contact
- Expert session webinars on all things college related and beyond: applications, resume, internships, school selection, job training, and much more
- Provide clarity on the entire college process

JOHN G. McCARTHY has been a leader in the late-stage college-planning process for more than fifteen years. He specializes in helping parents across the country avoid overpaying for college. John has personally overseen the training of more than 300 financial advisors from across the country to help them better serve their clients who are faced with late-stage college-planning problems.

John has been a vocal critic of the college-loan industry and it's predatory nature, crafting letters and lobbying for changes to the core structure of how college-loan laws are governed in this country.

John is a sought after speaker, both to families who are faced with the late-stage college problem and to financial advisors looking for better ways to serve their clients. John gives free workshops several times per month in and around the Pittsburgh area, at local high schools, libraries, community centers, and virtually anywhere he can share valuable information for parents faced with late-stage college-planning issues.

John shares tips, tactics, and strategies regularly through the PERFECT POSITION COLLEGE SOLUTION™ Letter. This is the undisputed number-one late-stage-college-planning-advice letter on the planet. Parents rave about how such a simple e-mail can transform their knowledge of the college system. They are taken from complete confusion about the college process to gaining a clear understanding of not only how the system works, but also how to take advantage of it and win the college game.

John chose his career path for several reasons. One, because it was instilled in him early in his life by his parents, George and Ann McCarthy, about the importance of getting the "best college education" one can afford. And two, because several of John's classmates at College of the Holy Cross were forced to leave school. Not because they didn't study or because they partied too much, but because their families didn't have a well-thought-out college gameplan.

What John quickly learned, when he researched how other families dealt with the college problem, is that there weren't any viable solutions available. So John partnered with a few of the leaders in late-stage college planning to shortcut the learning curve and arm himself with every possible tip, tactic, and strategy possible.

John is a firm believer that any parent, regardless of their background or financial circumstances, can send their child to college if they know how to play the college-planning game properly.

John is a graduate of College of the Holy Cross, in Worcester, MA and North Allegheny High School in Wexford, PA.

Since he's started educating parents on the college-funding process, John has helped hundreds of parents, including employees from these major companies and organizations:

EQT Corporation
Verizon Wireless
Allegheny Health Choices, Inc
Baierl Automotive
Ford
General Motors
University of Michigan–Ann Arbor
Oakland County (MI) School System

A native of Wexford, Pennsylvania, John is a life long fan of the Pittsburgh Steelers and Pitt Panthers football and basketball teams.

WHAT OTHERS ARE SAYING

"I've had the opportunity to work with John very closely over the last seven years and he's been fantastic. There are only a few people on the planet who I trust with helping me and my clients solve the late-stage college-planning process . . . and John is without a doubt one of them. Any advisor, or parent for that matter, would be much the wiser for having listened to and taken John's advice."

—Angie Grimm, Financial Advisor at Thompson & Thurman (Amarillo, TX)

"Since 2012, I've focused my practice on helping parents solve the many problems and challenges that arise when it comes time to send their children to college. John is one of the very few who truly understand this problem *and* has the knowledge on how to solve it. Nearly every day, he's sending me some kind of advice to help better serve my clients. I look forward to those little nuggets of knowledge. If you're thinking about working with John, don't hesitate. There are only a few like him. Get him while he's available."

—Chelsea Watkins, Founder, College Application Training (Los Angeles, CA)

"Six years ago, I made the decision to focus on becoming a late-stage college-planning specialist. And John is the guy I sought out to help give me the knowledge and the confidence to help families solve the massive challenge that paying for college can be. If you are an advisor or a parent that's thinking about working with John . . . don't think— just do it. John has the ability to take a financial situation that's complicated and sometimes hopeless and turning it around so that families can not only have a clear path to college but also still keep their other financial goals in line."

—Michael Budnick, Budnick Financial Group

"Financial advisors and parents alike should 100% be listening to John when it comes to solving the late-stage college-planning problem. There are just a few experts on this subject I seek to guide me and my clients . . . and John is right there at the top of the list. You'd be crazy not to listen to him and take action on any advice his gives on the topic of college planning. He's that good."

—Ryan Fleming, Vice President, Eagle College Planning

"Seven years ago, I made the decision to reinvent my business and I choose to become a late-stage college-planning expert. Fast forward to today . . . John is the guy who helped me the most to get me to where I'm at today. I've got a thriving financial services practice that's helped hundreds and hundreds of families across Michigan solve one of the trickiest financial problem parents are faced with today—late-stage college planning. If you're thinking about hiring or working with John, just do it. You'll be thanking me later."

—Jon Dault, Founder Circle of Wealth Financial Services

"I've made financial advising my profession for more than 20 years. And there are only a handful of people I trust in the financial service industry—John is on that short list. His advice has helped me grow a thriving practice and service the nearly one thousand active families our firm works with. I've had the opportunity to work with John closely for over 13 years. His integrity and knowledge of how to solve parent's college-planning challenges is second to none. You'd be best served to take his advice and run with it."

—John Shedenhelm, Founder, Eagle Financial Services

"My wife and I attended one of John McCarthy's free introductory seminars at our local library, in order to learn more about our options for funding college expenses for our daughter and son. Shortly after the seminar we met with John, who was invaluable in helping us navigate our way through funding for college, the financial-aid process, which included filling out and submission of our first FAFSA, and ways to minimize our Expected Family Contribution while at the same time mitigating tax impacts.

With John's expertise and help, my wife and I have been able to fund our daughter and son's college expenses without worrying about where the money was going to come from.

John has always been there for us throughout the past five years to promptly answer any questions or concerns that we have had. It is extremely important to know your options and have a solid plan in place to successfully fund your child's college education! I highly recommend John to any parents that are navigating the college-funding process for the first time."

—Carl Thomas Farmington Hills, MI

"John asked if I would be willing to write a short testimonial concerning the work he has done for us in the past five years. I warned him that first, I am not known for being a person of few words!

Also, because John has helped us and our sons in so many ways, it might be difficult to give him his due credits with only a few words. When our older son was a junior in high school, we attended a brief, one-hour introduction to the process at our local high school.

Although we are both college graduates, we knew that the career choices available for this next generation was much more expansive than when we made our career and college decisions. As we listened to the information presented at the meeting, we also realized that there was much more required documentation for college applicants.

We had saved for college costs, but those costs were also rapidly increasing.

We knew that we needed help from a professional "in the business," and the presentation convinced us that John's company was well equipped to help us to prepare to send both of our sons to college.

We talked with John McCarthy after the meeting and felt he would definitely meet our needs. He exceeded our expectations in all areas.

During our first meeting John began by laying out the plan of the various areas in which he could assist us, and prioritizing the tasks based on timing. These included forms that needed to be filled out, career and school choices, financial aid opportunities, and at the same time remembering that we had retirement goals and planning.

Yes, we had saved for college expenses, but without some direction we would either be in the situation of reducing our retirement fund or requiring our sons to take out loans because we would be requiring them to pay even more than originally planned (they were expected to pay some expenses as we were not planning on paying all costs for them). He strategized with us and presented options for us, allowing us to express our personal feelings as to how much risk or stability we wanted to incur.

He had the facts, but treated our opinions with respect and always listened to our feelings so that we would be comfortable with every decision *we* made with his professional direction and guidance. At the same time he met with our son and gave him tests that helped him in determining his strengths and weaknesses and likes and dislikes, then reviewed that information with him to help our son choose potential careers.

Then John researched various schools for these choices and discussed them with our son. John proved himself as a professional who was capable of establishing a rapport with adults as well as teenagers, and our son respected his opinion.

As forms were needed during our son's senior year, John clearly directed us on the information he would need from us, and he completed the necessary documentation in a timely manner.

As we saw our friends struggle with rejections and rewrites of the information, our information was ready early and correct with the first submission. Also, as our son applied for various schools, scholarships and grants, John was there to assist in document preparation as needed.

Our son's senior year was smooth, as we saw the nightmare many other families experienced. Having John there to lead us along and help step-by-step made our senior year experience smooth and direct. Our son happily went off to college, and we continued to work with John.

John is an intelligent person who is well-read and makes every attempt to know critical information that would impact our investments and decisions. Even better, if he does not have the answer immediately, he will admit that, and search for information and confer with his fellow professionals rather than giving incorrect information.

We have only known John through our professional relationship; however he is always interested in our personal lives. He is very personable and always willing to take time to answer any questions. We have never regretted our decision to work with John, and very openly refer others to him. We look forward to continuing our relationship with John, and also look forward to the day that our sons are "on their own" working at their careers and consulting with John for their future plans!

—Roxie Fittonneville, Ph.D. GM retiree Clarkston, MI

36010557R00084

Made in the USA
Middletown, DE
14 February 2019